IT'S SCIENCE!

Water

Water

Sally Hewitt

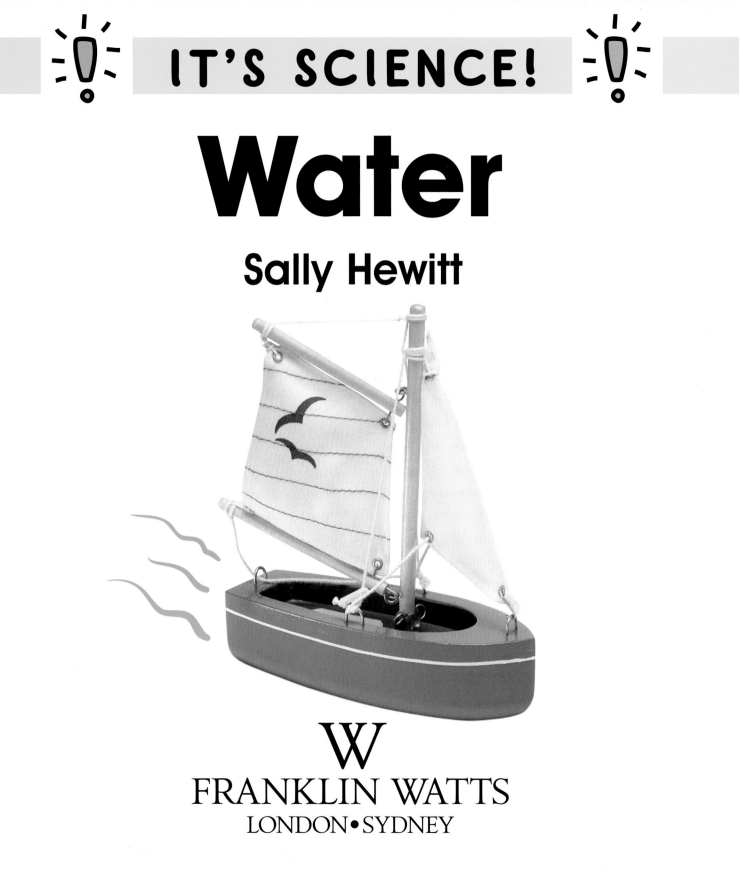

W

FRANKLIN WATTS
LONDON • SYDNEY

First published in 1999 by Franklin Watts
This edition published in 2001

Franklin Watts
96 Leonard Street
London EC2A 4XD

Franklin Watts Australia
56 O'Riordan Street
Alexandria, Sydney
NSW 2015

Series editor: Rachel Cooke
Designer: Mo Choy
Picture research: Sue Mennell
Photography: Ray Moller unless otherwise acknowledged
Series consultant: Sally Nanknivell-Aston

ISBN 0 7496 4272 6

Dewey Decimal Classification Number 553.7

A CIP catalogue record for this book is available from the
British Library.

Printed in Malaysia

Acknowledgements:
© Aqualisa Products Ltd. 1998 p. 16r; Bruce Coleman pp. 13tl (John Shaw),
26tr (Mark N. Boulton); Bubbles p. 14bl (Perry Joseph); James Davis Travel Photography p.19tr;
Eye Ubiquitous p. 6b (Dean Bennett); Robert Harding Picture Library pp. 13bl, 20;
Frank Lane Picture Agency pp. 8br (Mark Newman), 11tr (Foto Natura), 11br (Alan Williams), 22t (L.G.
Nilsson/Skylight); Natural History Photographic Agency pp. 11tl (Yves Lanceau), 11br (Alan Williams);
Oxford Scientific Films pp. 17bl (Ronald Toms), 25t (Max Gibbs);
Still Pictures pp. 12tr (Richard Pike), 12bl (Fred Bavendam).
Thanks, too, to our models Lily Dang, Gino Philip and Jade Stanford.

Contents

Wonderful water

Water is very useful! We use it every day for washing, drinking, cooking and in all kinds of different ways.

For many of us, water is very easy to find. We just turn on the cold tap for clean, fresh, cold water and the hot tap for steamy, hot water!

In some parts of the world finding water is not so easy. People have to walk a long way to collect it and then carry it back home again.

 THINK ABOUT IT!

Does water have a colour? Can you taste or smell it? Do you think it would be as useful if it had a strong colour, taste and smell?

How is water used for all these everyday jobs?
Could you do any of these things without using water?

 **TRY IT OUT!**

Draw a big glass of water. For just one day, draw one drop of water in the glass every time you turn on the tap, have a drink or use water in any way. Count how many drops of water there are in the glass at the end of the day.

Drinking

You need food to give you the **energy** to stay healthy, work hard and grow. But did you know you need water as well?

Your body is made up of a lot of water – more than anything else – so you need to drink plenty of water for your body to work properly. Your body is losing water all the time.

You lose water through your skin when you sweat on a hot day or after working hard.

You lose water when you go to the toilet.

You lose water every time you **breathe** out.

TRY IT OUT!

Go outside on a cold morning and breathe out. Tiny droplets of water in your warm breath make a mist you can see in the cold **air**.

When you feel hungry, your body is telling you that you need something to eat. When you feel thirsty, your body is telling you that you need to drink some water.

💡 THINK ABOUT IT!

What makes you feel thirsty?

Drinks are often made up of mixtures of water and other things, such as tea, sugar or juice. What is your favourite drink?

Did you know that there is also water in the food we eat?
Juicy fruit and crunchy vegetables have water in them.
Which of these foods do you think have a lot of water in them?

9

Water for life

All living things, people, animals and plants, need water. Without water there would be no life on Earth at all.

Plants take water up from the soil through their roots. It travels up the stem, into the leaves and flowers and every part of the plant.

Plants only keep a small amount of the water they take in. They lose most of it out through their leaves into the air.

TRY IT OUT!

Ask if you can pick a flower or take one from a vase. Leave it without water for a few hours and see how droopy it gets. Now put it in water. You should be able to see it change as the water flows up the stem into the leaves and flower.

Just like us, all other animals need water to live, even a fly. Pet owners need to make sure that their pets have plenty of clean, fresh water, especially after they have been for a walk or for a run on an exercise wheel!

 TRY IT OUT!

We often remember to put o seeds and nuts for birds, but they need water, too! Put out some water safely away from cats. Keep it clean and fresh every day. Watch the birds come for a drink and a bath

11

Water everywhere

Did you know that there is more water on Earth, the planet we live on, than land?

Most of the water on Earth is salty sea water. The sea is salty because rivers collect salt from rocks and soil as they flow over the land and carry it down to the sea.

Seaweed, corals, fish and all kinds of sea creatures live in the sea, but salty sea water is not good for us to drink.

💡 THINK ABOUT IT!

Salty foods like crisps make you thirsty. Would salty sea water make you thirsty, too? Try a sip of water with a little salt mixed in. What does it taste like?

Water that falls from the sky as rain is fresh, not salty. Fresh water is the water we drink.

 LOOK AGAIN

Look again at page 8. Why do we need to drink plenty of fresh water?

Springs of fresh water bubble up from under the ground. The water in streams, rivers and lakes is fresh water too.

It is so cold at the North and South Poles that fresh water there is always frozen as **ice**. Sometimes gigantic blocks of ice break away and float off into the sea. We call these blocks icebergs.

The water cycle

When it rains, puddles form on the ground. Later, these puddles dry up and the water seems to disappear. Actually, it turns into an invisible **gas** called **water vapour**. We call this change **evaporation**.

Evaporation is part of the **water cycle**. This is the way water on Earth is never lost. The same water goes round and round. Follow the circle around to see how the water cycle works.

Water vapour rises high into the air where it cools and turns into tiny water droplets. We call this change **condensation**.

Water is always evaporating – from the ground, rivers, lakes and oceans.

TRY IT OUT!

Put a little water in a bowl.
Leave it in the sun for a while until the water evaporates. How long does it take?
See how long it takes puddles to dry up after it rains.

Water droplets collect in **clouds**. They join together and fall as rain.

Rain falls and joins rivers and lakes. Some soaks into the ground.

River water flows back into the sea.

LOOK AGAIN

Look again at page 12 to find out why sea water is salty.

Some water is collected and stored in a **reservoir**. This water is cleaned in a water works and piped to our homes.

15

Clean water

It doesn't really matter how dirty you get, you can always have a bath or a shower and put your clothes in the wash and you will soon be clean again!

Clean water comes from the water works along underground pipes to your home.

When you turn on your tap, clean water flows out.

 **THINK ABOUT IT!**

How easy would it be to keep clean without using water? What could you use instead?

TRY IT OUT!

Find two glasses. After you have had a bath, fill one glass with dirty bath water. Fill the other with clean water from the tap. How is the water different in each glass? Would you drink the bath water?

Here are some of the things you might put in water when you use it to keep clean.

Washing powder

Do you know what happens to dirty water when you flush the toilet or pull out the bath plug?

The dirty water flows away along underground pipes to a sewage works. There, dirt is removed, harmful germs are killed and the clean water is put back into the rivers or reservoirs.

17

Liquid water

The water that flows out of your taps is **liquid**. It feels wet!

Water takes on the shape of any container it is poured into. Try pouring the same water from a glass jug into a mug, then a bowl and then into a bottle. See what happens to the shape of the water.

💡 THINK ABOUT IT!

What happens to water when you spill it out of a container?

Honey, oil and juice are liquids, too. They can all be poured. Can you think of anything else that is a liquid?

Gravity is a **force** that pulls everything downwards, including water. It is gravity that makes water flow.

Sometimes, water flowing over a waterfall is so powerful that energy from it can be used to make **electricity**.

 LOOK AGAIN

Look again at page 15 to see how water flows from rivers into the sea. Does it flow uphill or downhill?

TRY IT OUT!

Ask an adult to help you cut the top off a plastic bottle and make a hole near the bottom. Put a bowl under the hole to collect the water. Pour some water into the bottle and watch it flow out of the hole. Try again but put more water in the bottle this time. Does the water flow faster or slower?

Ice

A spoon, a cup, a jug, a cake and a log are all **solid**. Most of the things you see around you are solid. Did you know that water can be solid as well as liquid?

The freezer compartment in your fridge is very cold. If you put liquid water in the freezer it will **freeze** and become a solid called ice.

 TRY IT OUT!

Fill a balloon with water and tie it up. Fill some other containers (without lids) right up, too, and put them and the balloon in the freezer. Leave them until they are frozen. What shape has the solid ice taken? Does the ice take up the same space in the containers as the water did?

When it is very cold in the winter water from the clouds falls as icy snowflakes. The water in puddles and lakes freezes and becomes solid ice.

Tiny droplets of water in the air freeze and become frost on the ground and windows.

When the sun comes out and warms the air, snow and ice **melt** back into liquid water. Watch your frozen shapes melt back into liquid water when you leave them in the warm air. What happens to their shape?

 **LOOK AGAIN**

Look again at page 18 to find some liquids.
What differences can you see between a solid and a liquid?

Mist and steam

Did you know that the air you breathe has water in it? Air is a mixture of gases that you can not see. Water vapour is one of the gases in air.

We can't usually see water vapour. But sometimes chilly air turns it back into drops of water you can see and it becomes mist. Very thick mist is called fog.

👁 LOOK AGAIN

Look again at page 14 to find how water vapour gets into the air.

🖐 TRY IT OUT!

Wash some clothes and hang them outside to dry. What happens to the water in the clothes? Do they dry more quickly on a sunny or cloudy day? Does the wind make clothes dry any faster?

22

Next time you see a cup of tea or a kettle boiling or very hot water pouring from the hot water tap, look out for a white cloud rising off the water.

When water is heated up in a kettle, it boils and turns into very hot water vapour called **steam**. When the steam hits the colder air, it turns back into droplets of water that we can see.

When you have a bath, the air in the bathroom often becomes steamy from the hot bath water.

TRY IT OUT!

Steam condenses to form droplets of water on cold mirrors or windows. We say they have steamed up. You can draw pictures on the steamed up mirror. Wipe the droplets off with a tissue. Does the tissue feel wet?

Mix and stir

Water is very good for making mixtures.

⚡ TRY IT OUT!

Try making mixtures of water and different things like mud, sugar, paint, coffee and washing-up liquid. Stir them up well. What does the water look like now?

Leave the mixtures to stand for a little while.
Does the mixture look different from when it had just been stirred?

Some things seem to disappear completely when they are mixed with water. We say they have **dissolved** and call the mixture a **solution**.

24

TRY IT OUT!

Can you see white sugar when it is mixed with water?
Has it really disappeared?
Dip your finger in the solution and taste it.
Is the sugar still there?

Can you see the bubbles of air being pumped into the water in this fish tank? The pump is doing an important job because the air in the bubbles dissolves in the water so the fish and plants can breathe.

LOOK AGAIN

Look again at page 12. What is sea water a solution of?

25

Floating and sinking

It can be quite difficult to guess which objects will float in water and which will sink to the bottom.

Would you have guessed that a giant oil tanker floats and a tiny pebble sinks?

TRY IT OUT!

Collect some objects similar to these that are all kinds of different shapes and sizes and made of different materials.
Look at their shape. Do they feel heavy or light?
Guess which will float and which will sink.
Put them in water and try it out.
Did you guess right?

When you put something in water two things happen at the same time - the object pushes down on the water and the water pushes back up on the object.

 TRY IT OUT!

Find an old plastic bottle with its lid on – it may seem empty but in fact it is full of air. Now float it on water and try pushing down on it. Can you feel the water pushing it up? Fill the bottle with water and try floating it again. What happens now?

You can make the same piece of modelling clay float or sink.
Can you make it into a shape that sinks?
Try making it into a shape that floats.

A boat is a good shape for floating.

 THINK ABOUT IT!

Why do you think a little pebble sinks and a big balloon floats?

27

Useful words

Air Air is a mixture of gases we can't see but it is all around us. People, animals and plants need air to live.

Breathe When you breathe, you take air in and out of your lungs. Like other living things, we need oxygen, a gas in air, to live so we breathe all the time.

Clouds Clouds are formed when water droplets and ice crystals in the air collect together in a mass. Water falls from clouds as rain, hail or snow.

Condensation When water vapour cools it changes into liquid water. We call this change condensation.

Dissolve Some solids like salt and sugar dissolve in water. They mix in with the water and seem to disappear.

Electricity Electricity is a kind of energy. We use it to power lights, televisions and all kinds of other machines that need energy to work.

Energy Energy is what people, animals and machines need to give them the power to work. People get their energy from food.

Evaporation When a puddle dries up, the water in it changes from a liquid to a gas called water vapour. We call this change evaporation.

Force A force pushes or pulls an object. Wind and gravity are both natural forces.

Freeze When water becomes very cold it changes into solid ice. We say it freezes.

Gas The air all around us is made up of different gases. Gas does not have a shape of its own.

Gravity Gravity is an invisible force. It pulls everything towards the ground.

Ice When liquid water gets very cold, it freezes into a solid called ice.

Liquid Water, oil and juice are kinds of liquids. A liquid can be poured and does not have a shape of its own.

Melt When a solid is heated and turns into a liquid we say it melts. When solid ice becomes warm, it melts back into liquid water.

Reservoir A reservoir is a lake, often built by people, where water is stored before it is piped to our homes.

Solid Ice, a brick and a log are all solid. Solid things are neither liquid nor gas. They have a shape of their own.

Solution When a solid like salt or sugar dissolves in water, we call the mixture they form a solution.

Steam When water is heated up, it boils and turns into very hot water vapour called steam.

Water cycle The water cycle is the name given to the way water on Earth is always moving from the sea, lakes and rivers, to the sky as water vapour and clouds, and to the ground again as rain.

Water vapour When water is heated it becomes a gas called water vapour.

Index

About this book

Children are natural scientists. They learn by touching and feeling, noticing, asking questions and trying things out for themselves. The books in the *It's Science!* series are designed for the way children learn. Familiar objects are used as starting points for further learning. *Water* starts with water from the tap and explores the different ways we use it and the different forms it takes.

Each double page spread introduces a new topic, such as the water cycle. Information is given, questions asked and activities suggested that encourage children to make discoveries and develop new ideas for themselves.
Look out for these panels throughout the book:

TRY IT OUT! indicates a simple activity, using safe materials, that proves or explores a point.
THINK ABOUT IT! indicates a question inspired by the information on the page but which points the reader to areas not covered by the book.
LOOK AGAIN introduces a cross-referencing activity which links themes and facts through the book.

Encourage children not to take the familiar world for granted. Point things out, ask questions and enjoy making scientific discoveries together.